DOG FOOD COOKBOOK FOR ITCHING AND ALLERGIES

DR. WESLEY GLASGOW

TABLE OF CONTENTS

INTRODUCTION

Growing up, I was immersed in a world where the love for dogs coursed through my veins like a sacred river. From the tender age when my parents gifted me my first canine companion, Dan, I knew my heart belonged to the loyal, tail-wagging creatures that brought boundless joy into my life. Dan wasn't just a pet; he was my confidant, my playmate, and my constant companion.

As a young child, my adoration for Dan knew no bounds. I showered him with affection, and in my innocence, I believed that providing him with an abundance of treats and table scraps was the ultimate demonstration of love. Little did I know, my well-intentioned actions were setting the stage for a harrowing journey that would forever alter the course of my life.

After several blissful years spent in Dan's company, I noticed alarming changes in his health. He became lethargic, his once vibrant coat dulled, and he struggled to carry his weight. Concerned and bewildered, I sought the counsel of a veterinary professional, only to be met with a devastating diagnosis: Dan had developed diabetes as a result of his poor diet and excessive weight gain.

The weight of this revelation crushed me. How could I have unknowingly contributed to Dan's suffering? Guilt gnawed at my insides, and I vowed to do whatever it took to rectify my past mistakes and restore Dan to his former vitality.

Under the guidance of compassionate veterinarians, Dan's diet underwent a radical transformation. Gone were the days of indulgence and excess; instead, he was nourished with wholesome, nutrient-rich meals tailored to meet his specific dietary needs. Witnessing the miraculous metamorphosis that unfolded before my eyes, I was struck by the profound impact that proper nutrition could have on a dog's health and well-being.

From that pivotal moment onward, I embarked on a relentless quest to unlock the secrets of canine nutrition. Armed with boundless curiosity and an insatiable hunger for knowledge, I delved deep into the realms of veterinary science and culinary artistry, honing my skills and refining my craft with each passing year.

Today, after two and a half decades spent dedicated to the pursuit of canine culinary excellence, I stand before you not only as a seasoned veterinarian but also as a fervent advocate for the health and happiness of our four-legged companions. My name is Dr. Wesley Glasgow, and I am honored to share with you the culmination of my life's work: a meticulously curated collection of recipes designed to nourish, heal, and delight the palates of dogs afflicted by itching and allergies.

But before we embark on this culinary odyssey together, let me pose a few questions that I hope will stir the depths of your soul: What lengths would you go to ensure the well-being of your beloved furry friend? How do you envision the quality of their life, and what role does nutrition play in shaping that vision? And perhaps most importantly, are you ready to take the first step towards transforming your dog's health and vitality through the power of wholesome, thoughtfully crafted meals?

In the pages that follow, we will explore the myriad benefits of healthy eating for dogs, from bolstering their immune systems and enhancing their energy levels to promoting optimal digestion and skin health. We will also confront the sobering realities of unhealthy eating habits, shining a spotlight on the dangers and consequences that lurk in the shadows of ignorance and neglect.

But fear not, dear reader, for within the embrace of this cookbook lies the promise of redemption and renewal. By embracing the principles of balanced nutrition and embracing the recipes contained herein, you hold in your hands the key to unlocking a brighter, healthier future for your canine companion.

So, I invite you to join me on this transformative journey, where each meal is a testament to the unwavering bond between human and hound, and where love, compassion, and nourishment intertwine to create a symphony of healing and hope. Together, let us embark on a culinary adventure unlike any other, where every bite is imbued with the power to heal, uplift, and inspire.

Welcome to the Dog Food Cookbook for Itching and Allergies. Your journey begins here.

Contact the Author

Thank you for reading my book! I would love to hear from you, whether you have feedback, questions, or just want to share your thoughts. Your feedback means a lot to me and helps me improve as a writer.

Please don't hesitate to reach out to me through

glasgowesley@gmail.com

I look forward to connecting with my readers and appreciate your support in this literary journey. Your thoughts and comments are valuable to me.

Chapter 1
Understanding Canine Allergies

Canine allergies are a common concern among dog owners, impacting the health and well-being of their beloved pets. Allergies in dogs can manifest in various ways, including itching, skin irritation, gastrointestinal issues, and respiratory symptoms. Identifying and managing these allergies is crucial for maintaining the overall health and happiness of our canine companions.

There are three primary types of allergies that affect dogs:

1. **Environmental Allergies:** These are triggered by environmental factors such as pollen, dust mites, mold, and certain chemicals. Dogs may exhibit symptoms like itching, redness, sneezing, and watery eyes when exposed to these allergens.

2. **Food Allergies:** Food allergies occur when a dog's immune system reacts to specific ingredients in their diet. Common allergens include proteins like beef, chicken, dairy, and grains such as wheat and corn. Symptoms may include itching, gastrointestinal upset, chronic ear infections, and skin inflammation.

3. **Flea Allergies:** Some dogs are hypersensitive to flea bites, leading to an allergic reaction known as flea allergy dermatitis (FAD). Even a single flea bite can trigger intense itching and discomfort in these sensitive dogs.

Proper diagnosis of canine allergies is essential for effective management. Veterinarians may conduct skin tests, blood tests, elimination diets, or other diagnostic procedures to identify the underlying allergens.

Once allergies are diagnosed, managing them often involves a combination of strategies:

1. **Avoidance:** Whenever possible, minimizing exposure to known allergens can help reduce symptoms. For environmental allergies, this may involve keeping dogs indoors during peak pollen seasons or using air purifiers to reduce indoor allergens. In the case of food allergies, eliminating the problematic ingredients from the dog's diet is crucial.

2. **Medications:** Veterinarians may prescribe medications such as antihistamines, corticosteroids, or immunosuppressants to alleviate itching and inflammation associated with allergies. Flea control products can help manage flea allergies by preventing infestations.

3. **Allergy Shots (Immunotherapy):** In cases of severe allergies, allergen-specific immunotherapy (allergy shots) may be recommended. This involves administering gradually increasing doses of the allergen to desensitize the dog's immune system over time.

Importance of Proper Nutrition in Managing Itching and Allergies

Nutrition plays a crucial role in managing itching and allergies in dogs. A balanced and high-quality diet can support a healthy immune system, reduce inflammation, and improve skin and coat health, ultimately alleviating allergic symptoms.

When selecting a diet for a dog with allergies, consider the following:

1. **Limited Ingredient Diets:** Switching to a limited ingredient diet can help identify and eliminate potential allergens. These diets contain a minimal number of ingredients, making it easier to pinpoint and avoid triggers.

2. **Novel Protein Sources:** Opting for novel protein sources such as venison, duck, rabbit, or fish can be beneficial for dogs with food allergies. These proteins are less likely to trigger allergic reactions compared to common allergens like beef and chicken.

3. **Grain-Free or Grain-Inclusive Formulas:** While grain allergies are less common in dogs compared to other allergens, some dogs may still benefit from grain-free or grain-inclusive diets. However, recent research suggests that grain-free diets may be associated with an increased risk of heart disease, so it's essential to consult with a veterinarian when choosing a diet.

4. **Essential Fatty Acids:** Omega-3 and omega-6 fatty acids play a crucial role in maintaining healthy skin and coat. Supplementing the diet with sources of these fatty acids, such as fish oil or flaxseed oil, can help reduce itching and inflammation associated with allergies.

Chapter 2
Basics of Homemade Dog Food

Many pet owners opt to prepare homemade dog food as a way to provide their furry friends with fresh, nutritious meals tailored to their specific needs. While homemade dog food can offer several benefits, including control over ingredients and quality, it's essential to ensure that these meals meet the nutritional requirements of dogs. Here's a guide to the basics of homemade dog food, including nutritional requirements, ingredients, substitutions, and food safety tips:

Nutritional Requirements for Dogs

Before embarking on homemade dog food preparation, it's crucial to understand the basic nutritional requirements for dogs. These include:

1. Protein: Dogs require high-quality protein sources for muscle maintenance and overall health. Protein can come from animal-based sources such as lean meats (e.g., chicken, turkey, beef, fish) and eggs, as well as plant-based sources like legumes (e.g., lentils, chickpeas) and tofu.

2. Fats: Healthy fats provide essential fatty acids necessary for skin and coat health, as well as energy. Sources of healthy fats include animal fats (e.g., chicken fat, fish oil) and plant-based oils (e.g., olive oil, flaxseed oil).

3. Carbohydrates: Carbohydrates supply energy and fiber to support digestive health. Good carbohydrate sources for dogs include whole grains (e.g., brown rice, oats, barley), starchy vegetables (e.g., sweet potatoes, peas, pumpkin), and fruits (e.g., apples, berries).

4. Vitamins and Minerals: Dogs require a variety of vitamins and minerals to maintain overall health and function. These nutrients can be obtained from a balanced diet that includes a variety of ingredients. However, certain vitamins and minerals, such as calcium and vitamin D, may need to be supplemented, especially in homemade diets.

5. Water: Adequate hydration is essential for dogs' overall health and well-being. Fresh, clean water should always be available to dogs, whether they're eating commercial or homemade diets.

Ingredients and Substitutions

When preparing homemade dog food, it's essential to include a variety of ingredients to ensure balanced nutrition. Here are some common ingredients and possible substitutions:

1. Protein Sources: Lean meats (e.g., chicken, turkey, beef, lamb), fish (e.g., salmon, tuna), eggs, cottage cheese, and tofu can serve as primary protein sources. For dogs with allergies or sensitivities, consider novel protein sources such as venison, duck, or rabbit.

2. Carbohydrate Sources: Whole grains (e.g., brown rice, quinoa, barley), starchy vegetables (e.g., sweet potatoes, peas, carrots), and fruits (e.g., apples, blueberries, bananas) provide carbohydrates, fiber, and essential nutrients.

3. Fats and Oils: Animal fats (e.g., chicken fat, beef tallow) and plant-based oils (e.g., olive oil, coconut oil) are excellent sources of healthy fats. Avoid using excessive amounts of fat, as it can lead to obesity and other health issues.

4. Vegetables: Incorporate a variety of vegetables into homemade dog food for added vitamins, minerals, and fiber. Suitable options include leafy greens (e.g., spinach, kale), cruciferous vegetables (e.g., broccoli, cauliflower), and root vegetables (e.g., carrots, beets).

5. Supplements: Depending on the recipe and the dog's specific needs, certain supplements may be necessary to ensure nutritional adequacy. Common supplements for homemade dog food include calcium, vitamin D, omega-3 fatty acids, and multivitamins formulated for dogs.

Food Safety Tips for Homemade Dog Food

Maintaining proper food safety practices is crucial when preparing homemade dog food to prevent foodborne illness and ensure the safety of your dog. Here are some food safety tips to keep in mind:

1. Cleanliness: Wash your hands, utensils, and cooking surfaces thoroughly before and after handling raw ingredients to prevent contamination.

2. Fresh Ingredients: Use fresh, high-quality ingredients, and avoid using expired or spoiled foods.

3. Cooking Methods: Cook meats thoroughly to kill any harmful bacteria, and avoid feeding raw meat to dogs, as it may contain pathogens that can make them sick.

4. Storage: Store homemade dog food in airtight containers in the refrigerator or freezer to prevent spoilage. Use refrigerated food within a few days and frozen food within a few months.

5. Portion Control: Pay attention to portion sizes and feeding guidelines to prevent overfeeding, which can lead to obesity and other health issues.

6. Consultation: Consult with a veterinarian or a board-certified veterinary nutritionist before starting a homemade diet for your dog. They can provide guidance on recipe formulation, nutritional supplementation, and monitoring your dog's health.

Chapter 3
Allergy-Free Ingredients and Substitutes

For dogs with allergies, identifying and avoiding common allergens in their diet is crucial for maintaining their health and well-being. Here are some allergy-free ingredients and substitutes to consider when preparing homemade dog food:

1. Protein Sources:

    - Novel proteins: Opt for novel protein sources that your dog has not been exposed to before, such as venison, rabbit, or duck.

    - Limited ingredient diets: Choose commercial dog foods labeled as "limited ingredient" or "hypoallergenic," which typically contain a single protein source to minimize the risk of allergic reactions.

2. Carbohydrate Sources:

    - Alternative grains: Use grains that are less likely to trigger allergies, such as oats, quinoa, or millet.

    - Grain-free options: Consider grain-free carbohydrate sources like sweet potatoes, pumpkin, or lentils.

3. Fats and Oils:

- Fish oil: Supplement with fish oil, which provides omega-3 fatty acids without the risk of allergic reactions associated with other fat sources.

- Coconut oil: Use coconut oil as an alternative fat source, as it is less likely to cause allergies in dogs.

4. Vegetables and Fruits:

- Green beans: Substitute green beans for peas, which are a common allergen in commercial dog food.

- Blueberries: Offer blueberries as a low-allergy alternative to other fruits like apples or bananas.

Identifying Common Allergens in Commercial Dog Food

When selecting commercial dog food for your pet, it's essential to read labels carefully and be aware of common allergens that may trigger allergic reactions. Some common allergens found in commercial dog food include:

1. Protein sources:

- Beef

- Chicken

- Lamb

- Fish

- Dairy products (e.g., milk, cheese)

2. Grains:

- Wheat

- Corn

- Soy

- Rice

3. Other ingredients:

- Artificial preservatives, colors, and flavors

- Fillers (e.g., by-products, soybean meal)

Safe Alternatives for Allergic Dogs

If your dog is allergic to certain ingredients commonly found in commercial dog food, consider the following safe alternatives:

1. Homemade dog food: Prepare homemade dog food using allergy-free ingredients and substitutes tailored to your dog's dietary needs.

2. Limited ingredient diets: Switch to commercial dog foods labeled as "limited ingredient" or "hypoallergenic," which contain fewer ingredients and are less likely to trigger allergic reactions.

3. Novel protein sources: Introduce novel protein sources that your dog has not been exposed to before, such as venison, rabbit, or duck.

4. Grain-free options: Choose grain-free dog foods or recipes that use alternative carbohydrate sources like sweet potatoes, pumpkin, or lentils.

Tips for Introducing New Ingredients to Your Dog's Diet

When introducing new ingredients to your dog's diet, follow these tips to minimize the risk of allergic reactions and ensure a smooth transition:

1. Gradual introduction: Introduce new ingredients gradually, one at a time, and monitor your dog for any signs of allergic reactions or digestive upset.

2. Small portions: Start with small portions of the new ingredient and gradually increase the amount over several days to allow your dog's digestive system to adjust.

3. Observation: Keep a close eye on your dog for any signs of allergic reactions, such as itching, redness, vomiting, diarrhea, or changes in behavior.

4. Consultation: Consult with your veterinarian or a board-certified veterinary nutritionist before making any significant changes to your dog's diet, especially if they have a history of allergies or food sensitivities.

5. Patience: Be patient and give your dog time to adjust to the new ingredients. It may take some trial and error to find the right combination of foods that work for your dog's unique dietary needs.

Chapter 4

Comforting Breakfast Bowls

Oatmeal and Blueberry Bowl

- Cooking Time: 15 minutes

- Servings: 1

Ingredients:

- 1/2 cup rolled oats

- 1/4 cup fresh blueberries

- 1 tablespoon honey

- 1/4 cup plain Greek yogurt

Instructions:

1. Cook the oats according to package instructions.

2. Once cooked, let it cool slightly.

3. Mix in the fresh blueberries and honey.

4. Top with a dollop of plain Greek yogurt.

5. Serve at room temperature.

Nutritional Information: Calories: 250, Protein: 9g, Fat: 3g, Carbohydrates: 49g, Fiber: 5g

Sweet Potato and Turkey Bowl

- Cooking Time: 20 minutes

- Servings: 1

Ingredients:

- 1 small sweet potato, cooked and mashed

- 1/4 cup cooked ground turkey

- 1 tablespoon coconut oil

- 1 tablespoon pumpkin puree

Instructions:

1. Mix the mashed sweet potato and cooked ground turkey together.

2. Add coconut oil and pumpkin puree, stirring until well combined.

3. Microwave for 30 seconds to warm it up slightly.

4. Let it cool before serving.

Nutritional Information: Calories: 300, Protein: 15g, Fat: 10g, Carbohydrates: 40g, Fiber: 6g

Banana and Peanut Butter Bowl

- Cooking Time: 5 minutes

- Servings: 1

Ingredients:

- 1 ripe banana, mashed

- 2 tablespoons natural peanut butter

- 1/4 cup unsweetened applesauce

- 1/4 cup plain Greek yogurt

Instructions:

1. In a bowl, mix mashed banana and peanut butter until well combined.

2. Add unsweetened applesauce and mix thoroughly.

3. Top with a dollop of plain Greek yogurt.

4. Serve immediately.

Nutritional Information: Calories: 320, Protein: 10g, Fat: 15g, Carbohydrates: 40g, Fiber: 5g

Quinoa and Spinach Bowl

- Cooking Time: 20 minutes

- Servings: 1

Ingredients:

- 1/2 cup cooked quinoa

- 1/4 cup cooked spinach

- 1 tablespoon olive oil

- 1/4 cup cooked and shredded chicken breast

Instructions:

1. In a bowl, combine cooked quinoa and spinach.

2. Drizzle olive oil over the mixture and toss to coat.

3. Add cooked chicken breast on top.

4. Mix well and serve at room temperature.

Nutritional Information: Calories: 280, Protein: 20g, Fat: 8g, Carbohydrates: 35g, Fiber: 5g

Apple and Carrot Bowl

- Cooking Time: 10 minutes

- Servings: 1

Ingredients:

- 1/2 cup grated apple

- 1/2 cup grated carrot

- 2 tablespoons plain Greek yogurt

- 1 tablespoon honey

Instructions:

1. In a bowl, mix grated apple and carrot together.

2. Add plain Greek yogurt and honey, stirring until well combined.

3. Serve immediately.

Nutritional Information: Calories: 150, Protein: 5g, Fat: 0g, Carbohydrates: 35g, Fiber: 7g

Pumpkin and Rice Bowl

- Cooking Time: 15 minutes

- Servings: 1

Ingredients:

- 1/2 cup cooked brown rice

- 1/4 cup canned pumpkin puree

- 1/4 cup cooked lean ground beef or turkey

- 1 tablespoon flaxseed oil

Instructions:

1. Mix the cooked brown rice, canned pumpkin puree, and cooked ground beef or turkey together.

2. Drizzle flaxseed oil over the mixture and mix well.

3. Serve at room temperature.

Nutritional Information: Calories: 280, Protein: 15g, Fat: 8g, Carbohydrates: 35g, Fiber: 6g

Salmon and Potato Bowl

- Cooking Time: 25 minutes

- Servings: 1

Ingredients:

- 1/4 cup cooked and flaked salmon

- 1 small cooked potato, mashed

- 1 tablespoon olive oil

- 1/4 cup cooked green peas

Instructions:

1. In a bowl, mix the flaked salmon and mashed potato together.

2. Drizzle olive oil over the mixture and stir until well combined.

3. Add cooked green peas on top and mix gently.

4. Serve at room temperature.

Nutritional Information: Calories: 300, Protein: 20g, Fat: 10g, Carbohydrates: 35g, Fiber: 5g

Cottage Cheese and Berries Bowl

- Cooking Time: 5 minutes

- Servings: 1

Ingredients:

- 1/2 cup low-fat cottage cheese

- 1/4 cup mixed berries (such as strawberries, blueberries, raspberries)

- 1 tablespoon honey

- 1 tablespoon chopped fresh mint (optional)

Instructions:

1. In a bowl, mix low-fat cottage cheese and mixed berries together.

2. Drizzle honey over the mixture and stir gently.

3. Sprinkle chopped fresh mint on top if desired.

4. Serve immediately.

Nutritional Information: Calories: 200, Protein: 20g, Fat: 5g, Carbohydrates: 25g, Fiber: 5g

Yogurt and Carrot Bowl

- Cooking Time: 5 minutes

- Servings: 1

Ingredients:

- 1/2 cup plain Greek yogurt

- 1/4 cup grated carrot

- 1 tablespoon honey

- 1 tablespoon chopped walnuts

Instructions:

1. In a bowl, mix plain Greek yogurt and grated carrot together.

2. Drizzle honey over the mixture and stir gently.

3. Top with chopped walnuts.

4. Serve immediately.

Nutritional Information: Calories: 250, Protein: 15g, Fat: 10g, Carbohydrates: 30g, Fiber: 5g

Egg and Spinach Bowl

- Cooking Time: 10 minutes

- Servings: 1

Ingredients:

- 1 large egg

- 1/2 cup cooked spinach

- 1 tablespoon olive oil

- 1/4 cup cooked quinoa

Instructions:

1. In a skillet, heat olive oil over medium heat.

2. Crack the egg into the skillet and cook to desired doneness.

3. In a bowl, mix cooked spinach and quinoa together.

4. Place the cooked egg on top of the spinach and quinoa mixture.

5. Serve warm.

Nutritional Information: Calories: 300, Protein: 20g, Fat: 15g, Carbohydrates: 20g, Fiber: 5g

Chapter 5

Nourishing Main Courses

Turkey and Sweet Potato Stew

- Cooking Time: 30 minutes

- Servings: 4

Ingredients:

- 1 lb ground turkey

- 2 sweet potatoes, peeled and diced

- 1 cup green beans, chopped

- 1 cup carrots, sliced

- 4 cups low-sodium chicken broth

- 2 tablespoons olive oil

Instructions:

1. In a large pot, heat olive oil over medium heat.

2. Add ground turkey and cook until browned.

3. Stir in sweet potatoes, green beans, carrots, and chicken broth.

4. Bring to a boil, then reduce heat and simmer for 20 minutes or until vegetables are tender.

5. Let it cool before serving.

Nutritional Information: Calories: 300, Protein: 25g, Fat: 10g, Carbohydrates: 20g, Fiber: 5g

Salmon and Brown Rice Pilaf

- Cooking Time: 40 minutes

- Servings: 4

Ingredients:

- 1 lb salmon fillet, cooked and flaked

- 2 cups cooked brown rice

- 1 cup peas

- 1/2 cup carrots, diced

- 2 tablespoons coconut oil

Instructions:

1. In a skillet, heat coconut oil over medium heat.

2. Add peas and carrots, sauté until tender.

3. Stir in cooked brown rice and flaked salmon, mix well.

4. Cook for an additional 5 minutes, stirring occasionally.

5. Let it cool before serving.

Nutritional Information: Calories: 350, Protein: 30g, Fat: 15g, Carbohydrates: 25g, Fiber: 5g

Chicken and Vegetable Stir-Fry

- Cooking Time: 25 minutes

- Servings: 4

Ingredients:

- 1 lb boneless chicken breast, sliced

- 2 cups broccoli florets

- 1 bell pepper, sliced

- 1 cup snap peas

- 2 tablespoons sesame oil

Instructions:

1. In a large skillet, heat sesame oil over medium-high heat.

2. Add sliced chicken breast and cook until browned.

3. Stir in broccoli florets, bell pepper, and snap peas.

4. Cook for 10-15 minutes or until vegetables are tender.

5. Let it cool before serving.

Nutritional Information: Calories: 280, Protein: 30g, Fat: 10g, Carbohydrates: 15g, Fiber: 5g

Beef and Potato Casserole

- Cooking Time: 50 minutes

- Servings: 4

Ingredients:

- 1 lb lean ground beef

- 2 potatoes, peeled and diced

- 1 cup green beans, chopped

- 1 cup carrots, sliced

- 1 cup low-sodium beef broth

- 2 tablespoons olive oil

Instructions:

1. Preheat the oven to 375°F (190°C).

2. In a skillet, heat olive oil over medium heat.

3. Add ground beef and cook until browned.

4. Stir in potatoes, green beans, carrots, and beef broth.

5. Transfer the mixture into a baking dish and cover with foil.

6. Bake for 30-35 minutes or until vegetables are tender.

7. Let it cool before serving.

Nutritional Information: Calories: 320, Protein: 25g, Fat: 15g, Carbohydrates: 20g, Fiber: 5g

Tuna and Pasta Salad

- Cooking Time: 20 minutes

- Servings: 4

Ingredients:

- 2 cans tuna in water, drained

- 2 cups cooked pasta (choose whole grain for added fiber)

- 1 cup cherry tomatoes, halved

- 1/2 cup cucumber, diced

- 2 tablespoons olive oil

Instructions:

1. In a large bowl, combine tuna, cooked pasta, cherry tomatoes, and cucumber.

2. Drizzle olive oil over the mixture and toss to coat.

3. Serve at room temperature.

Nutritional Information: Calories: 280, Protein: 25g, Fat: 10g, Carbohydrates: 20g, Fiber: 5g

Lamb and Rice Stew

- Cooking Time: 40 minutes

- Servings: 4

Ingredients:

- 1 lb lamb meat, diced

- 1 cup cooked white rice

- 1 cup peas

- 1/2 cup carrots, diced

- 4 cups low-sodium beef broth

Instructions:

1. In a large pot, combine diced lamb meat and beef broth.

2. Bring to a boil, then reduce heat and simmer for 20 minutes.

3. Add cooked white rice, peas, and carrots.

4. Cook for an additional 10-15 minutes or until vegetables are tender.

5. Let it cool before serving.

Nutritional Information: Calories: 350, Protein: 30g, Fat: 15g, Carbohydrates: 25g, Fiber: 5g

Turkey and Barley Soup

- Cooking Time: 45 minutes

- Servings: 4

Ingredients:

- 1 lb ground turkey

- 1 cup barley, cooked

- 2 cups spinach, chopped

- 1 cup carrots, sliced

- 4 cups low-sodium chicken broth

Instructions:

1. In a large pot, cook ground turkey until browned.

2. Stir in cooked barley, spinach, carrots, and chicken broth.

3. Bring to a boil, then reduce heat and simmer for 30 minutes.

4. Let it cool before serving.

Nutritional Information: Calories: 300, Protein: 25g, Fat: 10g, Carbohydrates: 20g, Fiber: 5g

Chicken and Lentil Stew

- Cooking Time: 50 minutes

- Servings: 4

Ingredients:

- 1 lb chicken thighs, boneless and skinless, diced

- 1 cup lentils, cooked

- 2 cups sweet potatoes, diced

- 1 cup green beans, chopped

- 4 cups low-sodium chicken broth

Instructions:

1. In a large pot, combine diced chicken thighs and chicken broth.

2. Bring to a boil, then reduce heat and simmer for 30 minutes.

3. Stir in cooked lentils, sweet potatoes, and green beans.

4. Cook for an additional 15-20 minutes or until vegetables are tender.

5. Let it cool before serving.

Nutritional Information: Calories: 320, Protein: 30g, Fat: 15g, Carbohydrates: 20g, Fiber: 5g

Pork and Quinoa Skillet

- Cooking Time: 30 minutes

- Servings: 4

Ingredients:

- 1 lb pork loin, diced

- 1 cup cooked quinoa

- 1 cup broccoli florets

- 1 cup bell peppers, sliced

- 2 tablespoons olive oil

Instructions:

1. In a large skillet, heat olive oil over medium heat.

2. Add diced pork loin and cook until browned.

3. Stir in cooked quinoa, broccoli florets, and bell peppers.

4. Cook for 10-15 minutes or until vegetables are tender.

5. Let it cool before serving.

Nutritional Information: Calories: 350, Protein: 30g, Fat: 15g, Carbohydrates: 25g, Fiber: 5g

Fish and Potato Bake

- Cooking Time: 40 minutes

- Servings: 4

Ingredients:

- 1 lb white fish fillets (such as cod or tilapia)

- 2 potatoes, peeled and thinly sliced

- 1 cup green peas

- 1 lemon, sliced

- 2 tablespoons coconut oil

Instructions:

1. Preheat the oven to 375°F (190°C).

2. Grease a baking dish with coconut oil.

3. Layer thinly sliced potatoes at the bottom of the baking dish.

4. Place fish fillets on top of the potatoes.

5. Scatter green peas around the fish.

6. Top with lemon slices.

7. Bake for 25-30 minutes or until fish is cooked through.

8. Let it cool before serving.

Nutritional Information: Calories: 300, Protein: 25g, Fat: 10g, Carbohydrates: 20g, Fiber: 5g

Chapter 6
Satisfying Soups

Chicken and Rice Soup

- Cooking Time: 40 minutes

- Servings: 4

Ingredients:

- 1 lb boneless, skinless chicken breast

- 1 cup brown rice

- 2 carrots, diced

- 2 celery stalks, chopped

- 6 cups low-sodium chicken broth

Instructions:

1. In a large pot, bring chicken broth to a boil.

2. Add chicken breast and cook for 20 minutes or until cooked through.

3. Remove chicken from the pot, shred it, and set aside.

4. In the same pot, add brown rice, carrots, and celery.

5. Simmer for 15-20 minutes or until rice is tender.

6. Add shredded chicken back to the pot.

7. Let it cool before serving.

Nutritional Information: Calories: 300, Protein: 25g, Fat: 5g, Carbohydrates: 35g, Fiber: 5g

Beef and Vegetable Soup

- Cooking Time: 50 minutes

- Servings: 4

Ingredients:

- 1 lb lean beef stew meat, cubed

- 1 onion, diced

- 2 potatoes, peeled and diced

- 2 carrots, sliced

- 2 cups green beans, chopped

- 6 cups low-sodium beef broth

Instructions:

1. In a large pot, sauté onion until translucent.

2. Add beef stew meat and cook until browned.

3. Pour in beef broth and bring to a boil.

4. Reduce heat and simmer for 30 minutes.

5. Add potatoes, carrots, and green beans.

6. Cook for an additional 15-20 minutes or until vegetables are tender.

7. Let it cool before serving.

Nutritional Information: Calories: 350, Protein: 30g, Fat: 10g, Carbohydrates: 30g, Fiber: 6g

Turkey and Barley Soup

- Cooking Time: 45 minutes

- Servings: 4

Ingredients:

- 1 lb ground turkey

- 1 cup barley, rinsed

- 2 carrots, diced

- 2 celery stalks, chopped

- 6 cups low-sodium chicken broth

Instructions:

1. In a large pot, cook ground turkey until browned.

2. Add barley and chicken broth to the pot.

3. Bring to a boil, then reduce heat and simmer for 30 minutes.

4. Add carrots and celery.

5. Simmer for an additional 15 minutes or until vegetables are tender.

6. Let it cool before serving.

Nutritional Information: Calories: 320, Protein: 25g, Fat: 8g, Carbohydrates: 35g, Fiber: 7g

Fish and Vegetable Chowder

- Cooking Time: 40 minutes

- Servings: 4

Ingredients:

- 1 lb white fish fillets (such as cod or tilapia), diced

- 1 onion, diced

- 2 potatoes, peeled and diced

- 2 carrots, sliced

- 2 cups green peas

- 6 cups low-sodium fish broth

Instructions:

1. In a large pot, sauté onion until translucent.

2. Add diced fish fillets and cook for 5 minutes.

3. Pour in fish broth and bring to a boil.

4. Add potatoes, carrots, and green peas.

5. Simmer for 20-25 minutes or until vegetables are tender.

6. Let it cool before serving.

Nutritional Information: Calories: 280, Protein: 30g, Fat: 5g, Carbohydrates: 30g, Fiber: 8g

Lamb and Lentil Soup

- Cooking Time: 50 minutes

- Servings: 4

Ingredients:

- 1 lb lamb meat, diced

- 1 cup lentils, rinsed

- 1 onion, diced

- 2 carrots, diced

- 6 cups low-sodium beef broth

Instructions:

1. In a large pot, cook diced lamb meat until browned.

2. Add onion and cook until translucent.

3. Pour in beef broth and bring to a boil.

4. Add lentils and simmer for 30 minutes.

5. Add carrots and continue simmering for another 15-20 minutes or until vegetables are tender.

6. Let it cool before serving.

Nutritional Information: Calories: 350, Protein: 30g, Fat: 12g, Carbohydrates: 35g, Fiber: 10g

Pork and Potato Soup

- Cooking Time: 45 minutes

- Servings: 4

Ingredients:

- 1 lb pork loin, diced

- 2 potatoes, peeled and diced

- 1 onion, diced

- 2 carrots, sliced

- 6 cups low-sodium pork broth

Instructions:

1. In a large pot, cook diced pork loin until browned.

2. Add onion and cook until translucent.

3. Pour in pork broth and bring to a boil.

4. Add potatoes and carrots.

5. Simmer for 25-30 minutes or until vegetables are tender.

6. Let it cool before serving.

Nutritional Information: Calories: 320, Protein: 30g, Fat: 10g, Carbohydrates: 30g, Fiber: 6g

Chicken and Pumpkin Soup

- Cooking Time: 40 minutes

- Servings: 4

Ingredients:

- 1 lb boneless, skinless chicken thighs

- 1 cup pumpkin puree

- 2 potatoes, peeled and diced

- 2 carrots, diced

- 6 cups low-sodium chicken broth

Instructions:

1. In a large pot, bring chicken broth to a boil.

2. Add chicken thighs and cook for 20 minutes or until cooked through.

3. Remove chicken from the pot, shred it, and set aside.

4. In the same pot, add pumpkin puree, potatoes, and carrots.

5. Simmer for 15-20 minutes or until vegetables are tender.

6. Add shredded chicken back to the pot.

7. Let it cool before serving.

Nutritional Information: Calories: 280, Protein: 25g, Fat: 5g, Carbohydrates: 30g, Fiber: 6g

Turkey and Vegetable Soup

- Cooking Time: 45 minutes

- Servings: 4

Ingredients:

- 1 lb ground turkey

- 2 potatoes, peeled and diced

- 2 carrots, sliced

- 2 celery stalks, chopped

- 6 cups low-sodium chicken broth

Instructions:

1. In a large pot, cook ground turkey until browned.

2. Add potatoes, carrots, celery, and chicken broth to the pot.

3. Bring to a boil, then reduce heat and simmer for 30 minutes.

4. Let it cool before serving.

Nutritional Information: Calories: 320, Protein: 25g, Fat: 8g, Carbohydrates: 35g, Fiber: 7g

Beef and Barley Soup

- Cooking Time: 50 minutes

- Servings: 4

Ingredients:

- 1 lb lean beef stew meat, cubed

- 1 cup barley, rinsed

- 1 onion, diced

- 2 carrots, diced

- 6 cups low-sodium beef broth

Instructions:

1. In a large pot, sauté onion until translucent.

2. Add beef stew meat and cook until browned.

3. Pour in beef broth and bring to a boil.

4. Add barley and simmer for 30 minutes.

5. Add carrots and continue simmering for another 15-20 minutes or until vegetables are tender.

6. Let it cool before serving.

Nutritional Information: Calories: 350, Protein: 30g, Fat: 10g, Carbohydrates: 35g, Fiber: 8g

Salmon and Vegetable Soup

- Cooking Time: 40 minutes

- Servings: 4

Ingredients:

- 1 lb salmon fillets, diced

- 2 potatoes, peeled and diced

- 2 carrots, sliced

- 2 cups green beans, chopped

- 6 cups low-sodium fish broth

Instructions:

1. In a large pot, bring fish broth to a boil.

2. Add diced salmon fillets and cook for 5 minutes.

3. Add potatoes, carrots, and green beans.

4. Simmer for 20-25 minutes or until vegetables are tender.

5. Let it cool before serving.

Nutritional Information: Calories: 300, Protein: 30g, Fat: 8g, Carbohydrates: 30g, Fiber: 7g

Chapter 7

Snacks and Desserts

Peanut Butter Banana Bites

- Cooking Time: 15 minutes

- Servings: 8

Ingredients:

- 2 ripe bananas, mashed

- 1/4 cup natural peanut butter

- 1 cup rolled oats

Instructions:

1. Preheat the oven to 350°F (175°C) and line a baking sheet with parchment paper.

2. In a mixing bowl, combine mashed bananas, peanut butter, and rolled oats.

3. Mix until well combined.

4. Scoop tablespoon-sized portions of the mixture onto the prepared baking sheet.

5. Flatten each portion with a fork to form small discs.

6. Bake for 10-12 minutes or until golden brown.

7. Let them cool completely before serving.

Nutritional Information: Calories: 100, Protein: 3g, Fat: 4g, Carbohydrates: 15g, Fiber: 2g

Carrot and Apple Dog Cookies

- Cooking Time: 25 minutes

- Servings: 12

Ingredients:

- 1 cup grated carrots

- 1 cup grated apple

- 2 cups whole wheat flour

- 1/4 cup water

Instructions:

1. Preheat the oven to 350°F (175°C) and line a baking sheet with parchment paper.

2. In a mixing bowl, combine grated carrots, grated apple, whole wheat flour, and water.

3. Mix until a dough forms, adding more water if needed.

4. Roll out the dough on a floured surface to about 1/4 inch thickness.

5. Use cookie cutters to cut out shapes and place them onto the prepared baking sheet.

6. Bake for 20-25 minutes or until firm and golden.

7. Let them cool completely before serving.

Nutritional Information: Calories: 80, Protein: 2g, Fat: 1g, Carbohydrates: 16g, Fiber: 2g

Frozen Pumpkin Yogurt Treats

- Cooking Time: 5 minutes (plus freezing time)

- Servings: 8

Ingredients:

- 1 cup plain Greek yogurt

- 1/2 cup canned pumpkin puree

- 1 tablespoon honey

Instructions:

1. In a mixing bowl, combine Greek yogurt, pumpkin puree, and honey.

2. Stir until well combined.

3. Spoon the mixture into silicone molds or ice cube trays.

4. Place the molds or trays in the freezer and freeze until solid (about 2-3 hours).

5. Once frozen, remove the treats from the molds or trays and store them in an airtight container in the freezer.

6. Serve the frozen treats to your dog as a refreshing snack.

Nutritional Information: Calories: 30, Protein: 2g, Fat: 1g, Carbohydrates: 5g, Fiber: 1g

Blueberry Oatmeal Cookies

- Cooking Time: 20 minutes

- Servings: 12

Ingredients:

- 1 cup rolled oats

- 1/2 cup blueberries

- 1 ripe banana, mashed

- 2 tablespoons coconut oil

Instructions:

1. Preheat the oven to 350°F (175°C) and line a baking sheet with parchment paper.

2. In a mixing bowl, combine rolled oats, blueberries, mashed banana, and coconut oil.

3. Mix until well combined.

4. Drop tablespoon-sized portions of the mixture onto the prepared baking sheet.

5. Flatten each portion with the back of a spoon to form cookies.

6. Bake for 15-20 minutes or until golden brown.

7. Let them cool completely before serving.

Nutritional Information: Calories: 70, Protein: 1g, Fat: 3g, Carbohydrates: 10g, Fiber: 2g

Sweet Potato Chews

- Cooking Time: 3 hours

- Servings: varies

Ingredients:

- Sweet potatoes

Instructions:

1. Preheat the oven to 250°F (120°C).

2. Wash and peel sweet potatoes.

3. Slice sweet potatoes into thin strips, about 1/4 inch thick.

4. Place the sweet potato slices on a baking sheet lined with parchment paper, making sure they are not overlapping.

5. Bake for 2-3 hours, flipping halfway through, until the sweet potatoes are dried and chewy.

6. Let them cool completely before serving.

Nutritional Information: Calories: 50 per 1/4 cup serving, Protein: 1g, Fat: 0g, Carbohydrates: 12g, Fiber: 2g

Apple and Cinnamon Dog Donuts

- Cooking Time: 30 minutes

- Servings: 6

Ingredients:

- 1 cup unsweetened applesauce

- 1/4 cup coconut flour

- 1 teaspoon ground cinnamon

Instructions:

1. Preheat the oven to 350°F (175°C) and grease a donut pan.

2. In a mixing bowl, combine unsweetened applesauce, coconut flour, and ground cinnamon.

3. Mix until well combined.

4. Spoon the mixture into the donut pan, filling each cavity about halfway.

5. Bake for 20-25 minutes or until golden brown and set.

6. Let the donuts cool in the pan for 5 minutes before transferring them to a wire rack to cool completely.

7. Serve the cooled donuts to your dog as a special treat.

Nutritional Information: Calories: 40, Protein: 1g, Fat: 1g, Carbohydrates: 6g, Fiber: 2g

Frozen Berry Yogurt Pops

- Cooking Time: 5 minutes (plus freezing time)

- Servings: 6

Ingredients:

- 1 cup plain Greek yogurt

- 1/2 cup mixed berries (such as strawberries, blueberries, raspberries)

- 1 tablespoon honey

Instructions:

1. In a blender, combine Greek yogurt, mixed berries, and honey.

2. Blend until smooth.

3. Pour the mixture into popsicle molds or ice cube trays.

4. Insert popsicle sticks into the molds or trays.

5. Place in the freezer and freeze until solid (about 4-6 hours).

6. Once frozen, remove the pops from the molds or trays and store them in an airtight container in the freezer.

7. Serve the frozen yogurt pops to your dog as a cool and refreshing treat.

Nutritional Information: Calories: 30, Protein: 2g, Fat: 1g, Carbohydrates: 5g, Fiber: 1g

Peanut Butter Pumpkin Balls

- Cooking Time: 20 minutes (plus chilling time)

- Servings: 12

Ingredients:

- 1 cup canned pumpkin puree

- 1/2 cup natural peanut butter

- 2 cups oats

Instructions:

1. In a mixing bowl, combine pumpkin puree, peanut butter, and oats.

2. Mix until well combined.

3. Roll the mixture into balls about 1 inch in diameter.

4. Place the balls on a baking sheet lined with parchment paper.

5. Chill in the refrigerator for at least 1 hour before serving.

6. Store any leftovers in an airtight container in the refrigerator.

Nutritional Information: Calories: 70, Protein: 3g, Fat: 3g, Carbohydrates: 9g, Fiber: 2g

Frozen Banana Bites

- Cooking Time: 10 minutes (plus freezing time)

- Servings: varies

Ingredients:

- Bananas, sliced

- Peanut butter

Instructions:

1. Spread peanut butter on one side of each banana slice.

2. Sandwich two banana slices together, peanut butter sides facing each other.

3. Place the banana sandwiches on a baking sheet lined with parchment paper.

4. Freeze for at least 2 hours before serving.

5. Serve the frozen banana bites to your dog as a tasty and refreshing treat.

Nutritional Information: Calories: 50 per 1/4 cup serving, Protein: 1g, Fat: 2g, Carbohydrates: 8g, Fiber: 1g

Cheese and Oat Dog Biscuits

- Cooking Time: 30 minutes

- Servings: 24

Ingredients:

- 2 cups rolled oats

- 1 cup grated cheese (choose a low-fat variety)

- 1/2 cup unsweetened applesauce

- Water, as needed

Instructions:

1. Preheat the oven to 350°F (175°C) and line a baking sheet with parchment paper.

2. In a mixing bowl, combine rolled oats, grated cheese, and unsweetened applesauce.

3. Mix until well combined, adding water as needed to form a dough.

4. Roll out the dough on a floured surface to about 1/4 inch thickness.

5. Use cookie cutters to cut out shapes and place them onto the prepared baking sheet.

6. Bake for 20-25 minutes or until golden brown and crispy.

7. Let them cool completely before serving.

Nutritional Information: Calories: 50, Protein: 2g, Fat: 1g, Carbohydrates: 8g, Fiber: 1g

Chapter 8

Healthy Treats

Pumpkin and Oatmeal Biscuits

- Cooking Time: 25 minutes

- Servings: 24 biscuits

Ingredients:

- 1 cup canned pumpkin puree

- 2 cups rolled oats

- 1/4 cup coconut flour

- 1 egg

Instructions:

1. Preheat the oven to 350°F (175°C) and line a baking sheet with parchment paper.

2. In a large bowl, mix together pumpkin puree, rolled oats, coconut flour, and egg until well combined.

3. Roll out the dough on a floured surface to about 1/4 inch thickness.

4. Use cookie cutters to cut out shapes and place them on the prepared baking sheet.

5. Bake for 20-25 minutes or until golden brown.

6. Let the biscuits cool completely before serving.

Nutritional Information: Calories: 40, Protein: 2g, Fat: 1g, Carbohydrates: 6g, Fiber: 1g

Apple and Carrot Dog Muffins

- Cooking Time: 30 minutes

- Servings: 12 muffins

Ingredients:

- 1 cup grated apple

- 1 cup grated carrot

- 2 cups whole wheat flour

- 1/4 cup honey

- 1 egg

- 1 teaspoon baking powder

Instructions:

1. Preheat the oven to 350°F (175°C) and grease a muffin tin.

2. In a large bowl, mix together grated apple, grated carrot, whole wheat flour, honey, egg, and baking powder until well combined.

3. Spoon the batter into the muffin tin, filling each cup about 2/3 full.

4. Bake for 20-25 minutes or until a toothpick inserted into the center comes out clean.

5. Let the muffins cool in the tin for 5 minutes before transferring them to a wire rack to cool completely.

Nutritional Information: Calories: 90, Protein: 3g, Fat: 1g, Carbohydrates: 18g, Fiber: 2g

Blueberry and Banana Frozen Yogurt Bites

- Cooking Time: 2 hours (freezing time)

- Servings: varies

Ingredients:

- 1 cup plain Greek yogurt

- 1 ripe banana, mashed

- 1/2 cup blueberries

Instructions:

1. In a bowl, mix together Greek yogurt, mashed banana, and blueberries.

2. Spoon the mixture into silicone molds or ice cube trays.

3. Freeze for at least 2 hours or until solid.

4. Pop out the frozen yogurt bites from the molds.

5. Serve immediately or store in an airtight container in the freezer.

Nutritional Information: Calories: 30 per bite, Protein: 2g, Fat: 1g, Carbohydrates: 5g, Fiber: 1g

Spinach and Cheese Dog Treats

- Cooking Time: 30 minutes

- Servings: 24 treats

Ingredients:

- 1 cup cooked and chopped spinach

- 1/2 cup shredded cheddar cheese

- 1/4 cup oat flour

- 1 egg

Instructions:

1. Preheat the oven to 350°F (175°C) and line a baking sheet with parchment paper.

2. In a bowl, combine chopped spinach, shredded cheddar cheese, oat flour, and egg.

3. Mix until well combined.

4. Roll out the dough on a floured surface to about 1/4 inch thickness.

5. Use cookie cutters to cut out shapes and place them on the prepared baking sheet.

6. Bake for 20-25 minutes or until golden brown.

7. Let the treats cool completely before serving.

Nutritional Information: Calories: 35, Protein: 2g, Fat: 1g, Carbohydrates: 4g, Fiber: 1g

Peanut Butter and Banana Frozen Popsicles

- Cooking Time: 2 hours (freezing time)

- Servings: varies

Ingredients:

- 1 ripe banana, mashed

- 2 tablespoons natural peanut butter

- 1/2 cup plain Greek yogurt

Instructions:

1. In a bowl, mix together mashed banana, peanut butter, and Greek yogurt until smooth.

2. Spoon the mixture into popsicle molds.

3. Insert popsicle sticks into the molds.

4. Freeze for at least 2 hours or until solid.

5. Remove the popsicles from the molds and serve immediately.

Nutritional Information: Calories: 50 per popsicle, Protein: 3g, Fat: 2g, Carbohydrates: 6g, Fiber: 1g

Sweet Potato and Chicken Jerky

- Cooking Time: 3 hours

- Servings: varies

Ingredients:

- 1 large sweet potato, thinly sliced

- 1 cup cooked chicken breast, shredded

Instructions:

1. Preheat the oven to 250°F (120°C) and line a baking sheet with parchment paper.

2. Place the sweet potato slices and shredded chicken on the baking sheet in a single layer, making sure they don't overlap.

3. Bake for 2-3 hours or until the sweet potato slices are dried and crispy.

4. Let the jerky cool completely before serving.

Nutritional Information: Calories: Varies depending on size, Protein: Varies depending on size, Fat: Varies depending on size, Carbohydrates: Varies depending on size, Fiber: Varies depending on size

Coconut and Almond Flour Dog Biscuits

- Cooking Time: 30 minutes

- Servings: 24 biscuits

Ingredients:

- 1 cup coconut flour

- 1/2 cup almond flour

- 1/2 cup unsweetened coconut flakes

- 1/4 cup coconut oil, melted

- 1 egg

Instructions:

1. Preheat the oven to 350°F (175°C) and line a baking sheet with parchment paper.

2. In a bowl, mix together coconut flour, almond flour, coconut flakes, melted coconut oil, and egg until well combined.

3. Roll out the dough on a floured surface to about 1/4 inch thickness.

4. Use cookie cutters to cut out shapes and place them on the prepared baking sheet.

5. Bake for 20-25 minutes or until golden brown.

6. Let the biscuits cool completely before serving.

Nutritional Information: Calories: 40, Protein: 1g, Fat: 3g, Carbohydrates: 4g, Fiber: 2g

Carrot and Peanut Butter Dog Cookies

- Cooking Time: 20 minutes

- Servings: 24 cookies

Ingredients:

- 2 cups grated carrots

- 1/2 cup natural peanut butter

- 1 cup oat flour

- 1 egg

Instructions:

1. Preheat the oven to 350°F (175°C) and line a baking sheet with parchment paper.

2. In a bowl, mix together grated carrots, peanut butter, oat flour, and egg until well combined.

3. Roll the dough into small balls and place them on the prepared baking sheet.

4. Flatten each ball with the back of a fork.

5. Bake for 15-20 minutes or until golden brown.

6. Let the cookies cool completely before serving.

Nutritional Information: Calories: 50, Protein: 2g, Fat: 3g, Carbohydrates: 4g, Fiber: 1g

Turkey and Cranberry Dog Treats

- Cooking Time: 25 minutes

- Servings: 24 treats

Ingredients:

- 1 cup cooked turkey breast, shredded

- 1/4 cup dried cranberries

- 1/2 cup oat flour

- 1 egg

Instructions:

1. Preheat the oven to 350°F (175°C) and line a baking sheet with parchment paper.

2. In a bowl, mix together shredded turkey breast, dried cranberries, oat flour, and egg until well combined.

3. Roll out the dough on a floured surface to about 1/4 inch thickness.

4. Use cookie cutters to cut out shapes and place them on the prepared baking sheet.

5. Bake for 20-25 minutes or until golden brown.

6. Let the treats cool completely before serving.

Nutritional Information: Calories: 40, Protein: 3g, Fat: 1g, Carbohydrates: 5g, Fiber: 1g

Salmon and Sweet Potato Dog Bites

- Cooking Time: 40 minutes

- Servings: 24 bites

Ingredients:

- 1 cup cooked salmon, flaked

- 1/2 cup mashed sweet potato

- 1/4 cup almond flour

- 1 egg

Instructions:

1. Preheat the oven to 350°F (175°C) and line a baking sheet with parchment paper.

2. In a bowl, mix together flaked salmon, mashed sweet potato, almond flour, and egg until well combined.

3. Roll the mixture into small balls and place them on the prepared baking sheet.

4. Flatten each ball with the back of a fork.

5. Bake for 20-25 minutes or until cooked through and golden brown.

6. Let the bites cool completely before serving.

Nutritional Information: Calories: 40, Protein: 3g, Fat: 2g, Carbohydrates: 2g, Fiber: 1g

CONCLUSION

As we reach the culmination of our journey through the pages of the Dog Food Cookbook for Itching and Allergies, I am filled with a profound sense of gratitude and hope. Together, we have explored the boundless possibilities of canine cuisine, weaving a tapestry of nourishment, healing, and love that transcends the confines of mere sustenance.

Throughout these culinary adventures, we have delved deep into the heart of what it means to nourish our beloved four-legged companions, embracing the transformative power of wholesome, thoughtfully crafted meals to uplift their spirits and fortify their bodies against the ravages of itching and allergies. From tantalizing treats to sumptuous main courses, each recipe has been meticulously crafted with the well-being of our canine companions in mind, offering a symphony of flavors and nutrients designed to delight their palates and invigorate their souls.

But our journey does not end here, dear reader. As you close the final pages of this cookbook and embark on your own culinary odyssey, I urge you to carry forth the lessons learned and the wisdom gained, embracing the principles of balanced nutrition and compassionate care with every meal you prepare for your furry friend. Let each dish be a testament to the unbreakable bond between human and hound, a tangible expression of the love, devotion, and gratitude that flows between you and your canine companion.

As you embark on this new chapter of your journey, I invite you to share your experiences, thoughts, and feedback with me. Your insights are invaluable in shaping the future of this cookbook and ensuring that it continues to serve as a beacon of hope and inspiration for dog lovers around the world. Whether you found a particular recipe to be a resounding success or encountered challenges along the way, I welcome your honest review and encourage you to reach out with any questions, suggestions, or stories you wish to share.

Together, let us continue to champion the health and happiness of our furry friends, one nourishing meal at a time. Thank you for joining me on this extraordinary adventure, and may your kitchen be forever filled with the warmth of love, the joy of companionship, and the aroma of wholesome, delicious delights.

BONUS 1
Skin Care Tips for Dogs

A dog's skin is one of their most vital organs, serving as a protective barrier against environmental elements and pathogens. However, skin issues, such as itching, dryness, and allergies, are common concerns among dog owners. In this chapter, we will discuss essential skin care tips to help keep your dog's skin healthy and vibrant.

1. **Regular Grooming Routine**: Grooming plays a crucial role in maintaining your dog's skin health. Brushing your dog's coat regularly helps remove loose fur, dirt, and debris, preventing matting and reducing the risk of skin irritation. Additionally, regular grooming allows you to inspect your dog's skin for any signs of abnormalities, such as redness, inflammation, or lumps, that may require veterinary attention.

2. **Bathing Frequency**: While bathing is essential for keeping your dog clean, excessive bathing can strip away the natural oils that protect their skin, leading to dryness and irritation. The frequency of baths depends on your dog's breed, coat type, and lifestyle. Generally, most dogs benefit from a bath every 4-6 weeks. Use a mild, hypoallergenic dog shampoo formulated specifically for their skin type to avoid exacerbating skin issues.

3. **Moisturizing Routine**: Just like humans, dogs can experience dry skin, especially during the winter months or in arid climates. Consider incorporating a moisturizing routine into your dog's skincare regimen by applying a canine-friendly moisturizer or coconut oil to their skin, focusing on dry or flaky areas. Be sure to choose products that are free of artificial fragrances and harsh chemicals, as these can further irritate sensitive skin.

4. **Nutritious Diet**: Proper nutrition plays a significant role in maintaining your dog's skin health from the inside out. Ensure your dog's diet is balanced and provides essential nutrients, such as omega-3 fatty acids, vitamins A and E, and biotin, which are vital for healthy skin and coat. Consult with your veterinarian to determine the best diet for your dog's specific needs, especially if they have allergies or skin sensitivities.

5. **Regular Exercise**: Regular exercise not only benefits your dog's physical health but also contributes to their skin health by promoting circulation and oxygenation of the skin tissues. Engage your dog in daily activities such as walks, playtime, and interactive games to keep their skin and overall well-being in top condition.

6. **Flea and Tick Prevention**: Fleas and ticks are not only annoying pests but also potential carriers of diseases that can affect your dog's skin and overall health. Implement a comprehensive flea and tick prevention program that includes regular use of topical or oral preventatives, as well as environmental control measures like vacuuming and treating your home and yard.

7. **Allergen Management**: Identify and manage potential allergens in your dog's environment that may trigger skin allergies or irritations. Common allergens include pollen, dust mites, mold, and certain foods. Minimize exposure to these allergens by keeping your home clean, using hypoallergenic bedding and grooming products, and addressing any dietary sensitivities with your veterinarian.

8. **Routine Veterinary Check-ups**: Regular veterinary check-ups are essential for monitoring your dog's overall health, including their skin condition. Schedule annual wellness exams with your veterinarian, who can assess your dog's skin health, address any concerns, and recommend appropriate treatments or preventive measures tailored to your dog's individual needs.

BONUS 2

30 DAY MEAL PLAN

Day	Breakfast	Lunch	Dinner	Snacks
1	Peanut Butter Banana Bites	Apple and Carrot Dog Muffins	Salmon and Sweet Potato Bites	Frozen Pumpkin Yogurt Treats
2	Blueberry Oatmeal Cookies	Spinach and Cheese Dog Treats	Turkey and Cranberry Dog Treats	Frozen Berry Yogurt Pops
3	Carrot and Apple Dog Cookies	Sweet Potato Chews	Beef and Barley Soup	Peanut Butter Pumpkin Balls
4	Frozen Banana Bites	Coconut and Almond Flour Dog Biscuits	Chicken and Vegetable Stew	Sweet Potato Chews
5	Sweet Potato and Chicken Jerky	Cheese and Oat Dog Biscuits	Apple and Carrot Dog Muffins	Blueberry Oatmeal Cookies
6	Salmon and Vegetable Soup	Peanut Butter and Banana Frozen Popsicles	Spinach and Cheese Dog Treats	Frozen Banana Bites
7	Beef and Barley Soup	Turkey and Cranberry Dog Treats	Blueberry Oatmeal Cookies	Peanut Butter Banana Bites

8	Chicken and Vegetable Stew	Apple and Carrot Dog Muffins	Sweet Potato and Chicken Jerky	Frozen Berry Yogurt Pops
9	Cheese and Oat Dog Biscuits	Peanut Butter Pumpkin Balls	Carrot and Apple Dog Cookies	Coconut and Almond Flour Dog Biscuits
10	Peanut Butter and Banana Frozen Popsicles	Frozen Pumpkin Yogurt Treats	Spinach and Cheese Dog Treats	Sweet Potato Chews
11	Sweet Potato Chews	Frozen Berry Yogurt Pops	Beef and Barley Soup	Frozen Banana Bites
12	Coconut and Almond Flour Dog Biscuits	Peanut Butter Banana Bites	Salmon and Sweet Potato Bites	Blueberry Oatmeal Cookies
13	Spinach and Cheese Dog Treats	Blueberry Oatmeal Cookies	Chicken and Vegetable Stew	Peanut Butter and Banana Frozen Popsicles
14	Apple and Carrot Dog Muffins	Frozen Banana Bites	Turkey and Cranberry Dog Treats	Cheese and Oat Dog Biscuits
15	Turkey and Cranberry Dog Treats	Sweet Potato and Chicken Jerky	Coconut and Almond Flour Dog Biscuits	Frozen Berry Yogurt Pops
16	Chicken and Vegetable Stew	Cheese and Oat Dog Biscuits	Peanut Butter Pumpkin Balls	Apple and Carrot Dog Muffins

17	Blueberry Oatmeal Cookies	Frozen Pumpkin Yogurt Treats	Sweet Potato Chews	Salmon and Vegetable Soup
18	Frozen Banana Bites	Peanut Butter and Banana Frozen Popsicles	Spinach and Cheese Dog Treats	Beef and Barley Soup
19	Peanut Butter Pumpkin Balls	Coconut and Almond Flour Dog Biscuits	Apple and Carrot Dog Muffins	Frozen Berry Yogurt Pops
20	Sweet Potato and Chicken Jerky	Frozen Berry Yogurt Pops	Cheese and Oat Dog Biscuits	Blueberry Oatmeal Cookies
21	Frozen Berry Yogurt Pops	Peanut Butter Banana Bites	Peanut Butter and Banana Frozen Popsicles	Sweet Potato Chews
22	Beef and Barley Soup	Sweet Potato Chews	Coconut and Almond Flour Dog Biscuits	Chicken and Vegetable Stew
23	Peanut Butter Banana Bites	Blueberry Oatmeal Cookies	Apple and Carrot Dog Muffins	Turkey and Cranberry Dog Treats
24	Salmon and Sweet Potato Bites	Frozen Banana Bites	Peanut Butter Pumpkin Balls	Spinach and Cheese Dog Treats
25	Cheese and Oat Dog Biscuits	Chicken and Vegetable Stew	Frozen Berry Yogurt Pops	Peanut Butter and Banana

				Frozen Popsicles
26	Apple and Carrot Dog Muffins	Turkey and Cranberry Dog Treats	Sweet Potato and Chicken Jerky	Blueberry Oatmeal Cookies
27	Peanut Butter and Banana Frozen Popsicles	Coconut and Almond Flour Dog Biscuits	Beef and Barley Soup	Frozen Pumpkin Yogurt Treats
28	Sweet Potato Chews	Spinach and Cheese Dog Treats	Cheese and Oat Dog Biscuits	Salmon and Vegetable Soup
29	Frozen Pumpkin Yogurt Treats	Peanut Butter Pumpkin Balls	Frozen Banana Bites	Apple and Carrot Dog Muffins
30	Blueberry Oatmeal Cookies	Sweet Potato and Chicken Jerky	Peanut Butter and Banana Frozen Popsicles	Turkey and Cranberry Dog Treats

MEAL PLANNER JOURNAL

WEEKLY —

Meal Planner

Week of.

Monday	Tuesday	Wednesday
BREAKFAST	BREAKFAST	BREAKFAST
LUNCH	LUNCH	LUNCH
DINNER	DINNER	DINNER
SNACK	SNACK	SNACK

Thursday	Friday	Saturday
BREAKFAST	BREAKFAST	BREAKFAST
LUNCH	LUNCH	LUNCH
DINNER	DINNER	DINNER
SNACK	SNACK	SNACK

Sunday	NOTES:
BREAKFAST	
LUNCH	
DINNER	
SNACK	

WEEKLY —

Meal Planner

Week of:

Monday

BREAKFAST

LUNCH

DINNER

SNACK

Tuesday

BREAKFAST

LUNCH

DINNER

SNACK

Wednesday

BREAKFAST

LUNCH

DINNER

SNACK

Thursday

BREAKFAST

LUNCH

DINNER

SNACK

Friday

BREAKFAST

LUNCH

DINNER

SNACK

Saturday

BREAKFAST

LUNCH

DINNER

SNACK

Sunday

BREAKFAST

LUNCH

DINNER

SNACK

NOTES:

Meal Planner

Week of:

Monday

BREAKFAST

LUNCH

DINNER

SNACK

Tuesday

BREAKFAST

LUNCH

DINNER

SNACK

Wednesday

BREAKFAST

LUNCH

DINNER

SNACK

Thursday

BREAKFAST

LUNCH

DINNER

SNACK

Friday

BREAKFAST

LUNCH

DINNER

SNACK

Saturday

BREAKFAST

LUNCH

DINNER

SNACK

Sunday

BREAKFAST

LUNCH

DINNER

SNACK

NOTES:

Meal Planner

Week of:

Monday

BREAKFAST

LUNCH

DINNER

SNACK

Tuesday

BREAKFAST

LUNCH

DINNER

SNACK

Wednesday

BREAKFAST

LUNCH

DINNER

SNACK

Thursday

BREAKFAST

LUNCH

DINNER

SNACK

Friday

BREAKFAST

LUNCH

DINNER

SNACK

Saturday

BREAKFAST

LUNCH

DINNER

SNACK

Sunday

BREAKFAST

LUNCH

DINNER

SNACK

NOTES:

Meal Planner

Week of:

Monday	Tuesday	Wednesday
BREAKFAST	BREAKFAST	BREAKFAST
LUNCH	LUNCH	LUNCH
DINNER	DINNER	DINNER
SNACK	SNACK	SNACK

Thursday	Friday	Saturday
BREAKFAST	BREAKFAST	BREAKFAST
LUNCH	LUNCH	LUNCH
DINNER	DINNER	DINNER
SNACK	SNACK	SNACK

Sunday	NOTES:
BREAKFAST	
LUNCH	
DINNER	
SNACK	

Meal Planner

Week of:

Monday	Tuesday	Wednesday
BREAKFAST	BREAKFAST	BREAKFAST
LUNCH	LUNCH	LUNCH
DINNER	DINNER	DINNER
SNACK	SNACK	SNACK

Thursday	Friday	Saturday
BREAKFAST	BREAKFAST	BREAKFAST
LUNCH	LUNCH	LUNCH
DINNER	DINNER	DINNER
SNACK	SNACK	SNACK

Sunday	NOTES:
BREAKFAST	
LUNCH	
DINNER	
SNACK	

WEEKLY —

Meal Planner

Week of:

Monday

BREAKFAST

LUNCH

DINNER

SNACK

Tuesday

BREAKFAST

LUNCH

DINNER

SNACK

Wednesday

BREAKFAST

LUNCH

DINNER

SNACK

Thursday

BREAKFAST

LUNCH

DINNER

SNACK

Friday

BREAKFAST

LUNCH

DINNER

SNACK

Saturday

BREAKFAST

LUNCH

DINNER

SNACK

Sunday

BREAKFAST

LUNCH

DINNER

SNACK

NOTES:

WEEKLY —

Meal Planner

Week of:

Monday	Tuesday	Wednesday
BREAKFAST	BREAKFAST	BREAKFAST
LUNCH	LUNCH	LUNCH
DINNER	DINNER	DINNER
SNACK	SNACK	SNACK

Thursday	Friday	Saturday
BREAKFAST	BREAKFAST	BREAKFAST
LUNCH	LUNCH	LUNCH
DINNER	DINNER	DINNER
SNACK	SNACK	SNACK

Sunday	NOTES:
BREAKFAST	
LUNCH	
DINNER	
SNACK	

Meal Planner

Week of:

Monday	Tuesday	Wednesday
BREAKFAST	BREAKFAST	BREAKFAST
LUNCH	LUNCH	LUNCH
DINNER	DINNER	DINNER
SNACK	SNACK	SNACK

Thursday	Friday	Saturday
BREAKFAST	BREAKFAST	BREAKFAST
LUNCH	LUNCH	LUNCH
DINNER	DINNER	DINNER
SNACK	SNACK	SNACK

Sunday	NOTES:
BREAKFAST	
LUNCH	
DINNER	
SNACK	

WEEKLY —

Meal Planner

Week of:

Monday

BREAKFAST

LUNCH

DINNER

SNACK

Tuesday

BREAKFAST

LUNCH

DINNER

SNACK

Wednesday

BREAKFAST

LUNCH

DINNER

SNACK

Thursday

BREAKFAST

LUNCH

DINNER

SNACK

Friday

BREAKFAST

LUNCH

DINNER

SNACK

Saturday

BREAKFAST

LUNCH

DINNER

SNACK

Sunday

BREAKFAST

LUNCH

DINNER

SNACK

NOTES:

Meal Planner

Month of:

Sun	Mon	Tues	Wed	Thurs	Fri	Sat

Made in United States
Orlando, FL
05 June 2025

61879582R00052